Export Import Documentation Guideline

By

Gregory Taylor

1

Table of contents

Introduction

Chapter 3 ....Documents Required for Exporting

Introduction

Meaning, Benefits, and Drawbacks of Exporting and Importing

Goods and services are sent from one nation to another when they are exported. Similarly, purchasing or transporting goods and services from a foreign market into one's own country is an import. This is the easiest way for a company to get into international business because it doesn't require much

money to set up a production facility in another country; instead, it just needs distribution channels to successfully import or export goods.
A business can export or import in two ways:

• Direct imports and exports: In Direct Sending out/Bringing in, a firm straightforwardly manages the client/provider of the far off country and plays out every one of the customs, including shipment and supporting of labor and products.

• Import/export via indirect channels: A company uses middlemen to interact with a customer or supplier in indirect exporting and import. They don't deal with suppliers or customers directly. The majority of the formalities and work are completed with the assistance of middlemen, such as export houses, purchasing businesses or overseas customer offices, or wholesale importers in the case of import operations.

Chapter 1
Benefits of both exporting and importing

1. Simplest and easiest: When compared to any other method of entry, exporting and importing is the most straightforward approach. The absence of the need to establish and oversee a foreign business unit simplifies the procedure here.

2. Less expense: Less venture is expected on account of sending out/bringing in as it isn't required

for the undertaking to set up a specialty unit in the country they are managing.

3. Lower risk: The company is exempt from many of the risks associated with foreign investment if exporting or importing requires no or very little investment in the foreign country.

4. Resources Availability: Since resources aren't evenly distributed, every country needs to export and import goods from other

countries because no country can be 100% self-sufficient.

5. Improved Control: Due to the fact that there is very little involvement in the foreign country, exporting and importing can provide better trade control. There is no need to establish a unit in the foreign nation because everything is managed by the home nation.

Chapter 2
Importing and exporting have their disadvantages

1. Extra expense: Due to the fact that the goods will be shipped to various nations, there will be additional packaging and transportation costs, which is a significant limitation.

2. Regulations: Since foreign trade policies vary from country to country, it can be challenging for a business to follow all of the rules

and regulations in each country with which it deals.

3. Competition at home: The organizations engaged with sending out/bringing in need to confront extreme contest in the homegrown country because of the presence of homegrown dealers.

4. The Status of the Nation at Risk: Quality standards apply to goods that are shipped to other nations. The home nation's reputation is put into question if

low-quality goods are exported to any other nation.

5. Documentation: Every nation requires licenses and documentation for foreign trade when exporting or importing, which can sometimes become frustrating.

6. Multitasking: Multitasking is a big part of running a business across borders, which can be hectic for a company.

Chapter 3
Documents Required for Exporting

You've heard people talk about how to do the sexy part of exporting—the research, the schmoozing, the traveling, and all the marketing and sales stuff people think of when they think of international trade's glitz.

However, I want to discuss the less glamorous aspect of exporting: the fundamental export paperwork needed for international shipping. It's the work you need to do, and you need to do it right, to sell products and make money. I'd say that the less sexy aspects of exporting are more important than the more sexy ones, but maybe that's because I've been concentrating on them for more than 25 years.

In light of this, here are 11 standard export shipping documents that you must comprehend to succeed.

Proforma Invoice, Commercial Invoice, Packing List, Certificates of Origin, Free Sale Certificate, Shipper's Instruction, Ocean Bill of Lading, Dangerous Goods Forms, and Bank Draft

1. Proforma Invoice In a typical export exchange, the moment you receive an inquiry about one or more of your products marks the beginning of everything. That request might incorporate a solicitation for a citation.

You probably have a standard quotation form that you can use if the inquiry came from a domestic prospect. Be that as it may, in a global exchange, your statement would be given as a proforma receipt. That is on the grounds that your global possibility might require a proforma receipt to sort out for supporting, to open a letter of credit, to apply for the legitimate import licenses from there, the sky is the limit.

On the off chance that the request came from a homegrown possibility, you most likely have a standard citation structure to utilize. However, your quote would be provided as a proforma invoice in an international transaction. This is due to the fact that your international client may require a proforma invoice in order to obtain financing, open a letter of credit, and apply for the appropriate import licenses, among other things.

A proforma receipt seems to be a business receipt, and on the off chance that you complete it accurately, they will be very much quite like. A proforma receipt indicates the accompanying:

• Both parties involved in the transaction.

• A comprehensive description of the products.

• The goods' classification according to the Harmonized System.

• The cost.

• The sale's payment term, which is typically represented by one of the eleven current Incoterms.

• The specifics of the delivery, such as how and where the goods will be delivered and the price.

• The currency utilized in the quote, whether dollars from the United States or another currency.

Make certain to date your proforma receipt and incorporate a lapse date. Set a specific time frame for your quote to reduce your risk because the export process can be very volatile.

2. Commercial Invoice Following the receipt of your international prospect's order and the sending of a proforma invoice, you must prepare your goods for shipping, including the necessary paperwork. Of those archives, the business receipt is one of the most significant.

The bulk of the information regarding the entire export transaction, from beginning to end, can be found in the commercial invoice.

I frequently get inquiries from individuals who see this example business receipt and can't help thinking about why it appears to be so unique from the solicitations their organization utilizes for homegrown orders. Keep in mind that the invoices you create using your company's ERP or accounting system are not export invoices but rather invoices for accounting purposes.

Although the commercial invoice should include additional information that you were unaware of before, it may resemble the proforma invoice that you initially sent to your customer as a quote. You probably also have an order number, a purchase order number, or some other customer reference number once you have the commercial invoice; You might also have additional payment and banking details.

Include any relevant information about marine insurance as well as any other information that will guarantee your customer's full payment and prompt delivery of the goods.

3. Packing List An export packing list may be more in-depth than a domestic shipping packing list or packing slip. The following applications are possible with it:

•Your cargo forwarder may utilize the data on the pressing rundown to make the bills of filling for the shipment.

• When applying for a letter of credit, you may be required to submit a comprehensive packing list to a bank.

• The packing list can be used by U.S. and destination country customs officials to locate particular packed items they wish to examine. Instead of having to search the entire shipment, it's much better if they know which box or pallet to open.

The pressing rundown distinguishes things in the shipment and incorporates the net and gross weight and aspects of the bundles in both U.S. supreme and metric estimations. It identifies any special instructions for ensuring the safe delivery of the goods to their final destination as well as any markings that may be found on the packages.

A packing list is required to file an insurance claim if cargo is lost or damaged, and it is also used if the exporter and the carrier disagree about the cargo's weight or measurement.

4. Certificates of Origin In order to determine where goods originated, some nations require a certificate of origin. Most of the time, a semi-official organization, like a chamber of commerce or a country's consulate, must sign these certificates of origin. Even if you have included information about the country of origin on your commercial invoice, a certificate of origin may still be required.

In most cases, a chamber of commerce will either require you to be a member or charge you a fee to stamp and sign your certificate. A completed form must be delivered to the chamber office, where it will be stamped and signed on your behalf.

More and more businesses are relying on electronic certificates of origin (eCO) for their shipments instead of the time-consuming procedures of using costly courier services or hand-delivering certificates of origin to chambers of commerce for certification. An eCO can be registered with the

International Chamber of Commerce for added credibility, allows you to deliver the certificate electronically to the importer, and is typically quicker to process.

Country-Specific Certificates

There are country-specific certificates of origin in addition to the standard certificate of origin form. The US presently has consented to 14 streamlined commerce arrangements with 20 distinct nations in which U.S. products are qualified for diminished or zero obligation rates when brought into those nations. The United States is included in some free trade agreements, such as the United States-Central America-Dominican Republic Free Trade Agreement (CAFTA-DR). In our article, "When to Use a Certificate of Origin Form for Your Exports," we provide links to certificates that are specific to each country.

The NAFTA agreement between the three nations was replaced by the United States, Mexico, and

Canada Agreement (USMCA) on July 1, 2020.

5. Certificate of Free Sale—also known as a "Certificate to Foreign Governments" or "Certificate for Export"—is proof that a product—such as food, cosmetics, biologics, or medical devices—is legally sold or distributed in the open market, freely and without restrictions, and that the regulatory authorities in the country of origin (the United States) have approved it.

When you register a new product in a country, you use a Certificate of Free Sale. By saying, "This is a new thing I'm going to start importing, and here are my support documents that confirm this product(s) is legal to sell in the country of manufacture," you are effectively informing the customs authority in that nation.

You can easily apply for a Certificate of Free Sale online— registering is completely free—if an international customer requests one.

6. Shipper's Instruction Letter
Your freight forwarder is one of
the most important people you'll
work with during the export
process. He or she usually works
with a carrier to transport your
goods and makes sure you've taken
care of everything.

Either you, as the exporter,
employ a freight forwarder to
work for you, or, in the case of a
routed export transaction, the
buyer employs a freight forwarder,
depending on your agreed-upon

terms of sale (remember, that is typically the Incoterm you select).

You must provide a Shipper's Letter of Instruction (SLI) with all of the information necessary to move your goods successfully, regardless of who hired the forwarder.

I frequently depict the SLI as a cover notice for your other product desk work. The SLI may include a limited Power of Attorney that grants the forwarder authority to act on your behalf for this shipment, depending on whether or not they work for you.

AES Concerns The SLI may also grant the forwarder permission to electronically file the export information through the Automated Export System (AES) based on who hired the forwarder. Most products esteemed at more than $2,500 per thing should be submitted to customs by means of AES, which makes documenting through AES a significant thought for some exporters.

In the event that the cargo forwarder is employed by the purchaser, the forwarder ordinarily does the AES recording. Regardless of whether you, as the vender, recruit the forwarder, you might pay the forwarder to do the AES recording for your sake.

In either case, you are legally required to provide certain data elements to the forwarder for filing purposes even if you are not performing the AES filing yourself; Usually, this is done with SLI. Aside from that, I am of the firm opinion that you, as the exporter, ought to almost always be the party that files the AES, even in a routed export transaction in which the buyer chooses a forwarder.

It's easy to record the archives required for transportation through AES, and doing it without anyone else's help gives you more command over the cycle. Increasingly more of our clients are taking care of each and every commodity shipment for simply that explanation

Nonetheless, I comprehend that many organizations really do depend on a cargo forwarder for their AES filings, so a precisely finished SLI is vital.

7. Inland Bill of Replenishing

An inland bill of replenishing is much of the time the primary transportation record expected for global delivery made for your commodity. You can either make it yourself or have the inland carrier prepare it for you. It is a carriage contract that specifies the destination of the goods between the shipper and the exporter; It also serves as proof that the goods were picked up for you.

The buyer does not typically receive the inland bill of lading when shipping internationally. Instead, it is sent to the international shipping company or, if not sent directly to the shipping company, to a forwarder, warehouse, or other third party, who will then send your goods to the shipping company when they are ready.

8. Ocean Bill of Lading You will require an ocean bill of lading if your goods are being shipped by ocean vessel. Both a contract of carriage and a title document for the cargo can be found in an ocean bill of lading. Two kinds exist:

Straight Bill of Filling
A straight bill of filling is committed to a particular recipient and isn't debatable. By presenting the carrier with a signed

and original bill of lading, the consignee takes possession of the goods.

Debatable Bill of Replenishing
A debatable bill of replenishing is dispatched "to arrange" or "to request of transporter" and is endorsed by the transporter and shipped off a bank in the purchaser's country. Until the requirements for a documentary collection or a letter of credit have been met, the bank keeps the original bill of lading.

9. An air waybill is needed to ship goods on a plane. The International Air Transport Association (IATA) distributes this carriage contract between the shipper and the carrier. Not at all like a sea bill of replenishing, an air waybill can't be debatable.

A bill of lading serves a different purpose than an air waybill does:

• A receipt of goods is an air waybill; It is sent by the agent or carrier to indicate the location of delivery.

• A title document for goods is a bill of lading. It is a receipt issued by the shipping company with a promise to only deliver the goods to the party to whom the bill of lading is addressed at the destination.

10. Forms for Dangerous Goods If the International Air Transport Association (IATA) or the International Maritime Organization (IMO) consider your products to be dangerous goods, you must include the

appropriate dangerous goods form with your shipment. It can be difficult to ship hazardous goods or materials. In order to properly package, label, and document these shipments, you need to train the appropriate employees at your business before you do it.

For air shipments, the Shipper's Declaration for Dangerous Goods form from the IATA is required. For ocean shipments, there is a different version of the form. Again, these forms need to be filled out by a trained person who knows how to ship dangerous goods.

11. Bank Draft In international sales, a bank draft is a crucial component for transferring control of exported goods from the seller to the buyer in exchange for funds. Because the seller attaches a variety of documents to a bank draft and a cover letter, it is frequently referred to as a documentary collection.

Typically, the seller's bank will send the bank draft and any related documents to the buyer's bank or another bank in the buyer's country through a freight forwarder. The seller's bank receives the funds and the documents from the buyer's bank when the buyer authorizes payment for the goods.

A transmittal letter describing the bank draft transaction, including the types of additional documents and payment instructions, may or may not be included in the draft.

www.ingramcontent.com/pod-product-compliance
Lightning Source LLC
Chambersburg PA
CBHW062304290526
45794CB00006B/2690